# MznLnx

*Missing Links Exam Preps*

Exam Prep for

## Advanced Calculus

### Folland, 1st Edition

The MznLnx Exam Prep is your link from the texbook and lecture to your exams.
The MznLnx Exam Preps are unauthorized and comprehensive reviews of your textbooks.

All material provided by MznLnx and Rico Publications (c) 2010
Textbook publishers and textbook authors do not particpate in or contribute to these reviews.

# MznLnx

## Rico Publications

*Exam Prep for Advanced Calculus*
1st Edition
Folland

*Publisher:* Raymond Houge
*Assistant Editor:* Michael Rouger
*Text and Cover Designer:* Lisa Buckner
*Marketing Manager:* Sara Swagger
*Project Manager, Editorial Production:* Jerry Emerson
*Art Director:* Vernon Lowerui

*Product Manager:* Dave Mason
*Editorial Assitant:* Rachel Guzmanji
*Pedagogy:* Debra Long
*Cover Image:* Jim Reed/Getty Images
*Text and Cover Printer:* City Printing, Inc.
*Compositor:* Media Mix, Inc.

(c) 2010 Rico Publications
ALL RIGHTS RESERVED. No part of this work
covered by the copyright may be reproduced or
used in any form or by an means--graphic, electronic,
or mechanical, including photocopying, recording,
taping, Web distribution, information storage, and
retrieval systems, or in any other manner--without the
written permission of the publisher.

Printed in the United States
ISBN:

For more information about our products, contact us at:
Dave.Mason@RicoPublications.com

For permission to use material from this text or
product, submit a request online to:
Dave.Mason@RicoPublications.com

# Contents

**CHAPTER 1**
*Setting the Stage* — 1

**CHAPTER 2**
*Differential Calculus* — 13

**CHAPTER 3**
*The Implicit Function Theorem and Its Applications* — 21

**CHAPTER 4**
*Integral Calculus* — 23

**CHAPTER 5**
*Line and Surface Integrals; Vector Analysis* — 29

**CHAPTER 6**
*Infinite Series* — 38

**CHAPTER 7**
*Functions Defined by Series and Integrals* — 46

**CHAPTER 8**
*Fourier Series* — 54

**ANSWER KEY** — 62

# TO THE STUDENT

## COMPREHENSIVE

The *MznLnx* Exam Prep series is designed to help you pass your exams. Editors at MznLnx review your textbooks and then prepare these practice exams to help you master the textbook material. Unlike study guides, workbooks, and practice tests provided by the texbook publisher and textbook authors, *MznLnx* gives you **all** of the material in each chapter in exam form, not just samples, so you can be sure to nail your exam.

## MECHANICAL

The MznLnx Exam Prep series creates exams that will help you learn the subject matter as well as test you on your understanding. Each question is designed to help you master the concept. Just working through the exams, you gain an understanding of the subject--its a simple mechanical process that produces success.

## INTEGRATED STUDY GUIDE AND REVIEW

MznLnx is not just a set of exams designed to test you, its also a comprehensive review of the subject content. Each exam question is also a review of the concept, making sure that you will get the answer correct without having to go to other sources of material. You learn as you go! Its the easiest way to pass an exam.

## HUMOR

Studying can be tedious and dry. MznLnx's instructional design includes moderate humor within the exam questions on occassion, to break the tedium and revitalize the brain

## Chapter 1. Setting the Stage

1. _____ is a type of motion in which the velocity of an object changes equal amounts in equal time periods. An example of an object having _____ would be a ball rolling down a ramp. The object picks up velocity as it goes down the ramp with equal changes in time.
    a. ALGOR
    b. Uniform Acceleration
    c. AUSM
    d. ACTRAN

2. In mathematics, the _____ of a non-negative integer n, denoted by n!, is the product of all positive integers less than or equal to n. For example,

$$5! = 1 \times 2 \times 3 \times 4 \times 5 = 120$$

and

$$6! = 1 \times 2 \times 3 \times 4 \times 5 \times 6 = 720.$$

The notation n! was introduced by Christian Kramp in 1808.

The _____ function is formally defined by

$$n! = \prod_{k=1}^{n} k \qquad \forall n \in \mathbb{N}$$

or recursively defined by

$$n! = \begin{cases} n \leq 1 & 1 \\ n > 1 & n(n-1)! \end{cases} \qquad \forall n \in \mathbb{N}.$$

Both of the above definitions incorporate the instance

$$0! = 1$$

as an instance of the fact that the product of no numbers at all is 1.

## Chapter 1. Setting the Stage

   a. Factorial
   b. Constraint counting
   c. BDDC
   d. 15 theorem

3. In metric topology and related fields of mathematics, a set U is called _____ if, intuitively speaking, starting from any point x in U one can move by a small amount in any direction and still be in the set U. In other words, the distance between any point x in U and the edge of U is always greater than zero.

As an example, consider the _____ interval (0, 1) consisting of all real numbers x with 0 < x < 1. Here, the topology is the usual topology on the real line. We can look at this in two ways.

   a. AUSM
   b. ACTRAN
   c. ALGOR
   d. Open

4. In mathematics, the complex numbers are an extension of the real numbers obtained by adjoining an imaginary unit, denoted i.

Every _____ can be written in the form a + bi, where a and b are real numbers called the real part and the imaginary part of the _____, respectively.

Complex numbers are a field, and thus have addition, subtraction, multiplication, and division operations. These operations extend the corresponding operations on real numbers, although with a number of additional elegant and useful properties, e.g., negative real numbers can be obtained by squaring complex (imaginary) numbers.

   a. Filled Julia set
   b. Conjugated line
   c. Real part
   d. Complex number

5. In mathematics, the _____ (or replacement set) of a given function is the set of 'input' values for which the function is defined. For instance, the _____ of cosine would be all real numbers, while the _____ of the square root would be only numbers greater than or equal to 0 (ignoring complex numbers in both cases.) In a representation of a function in a xy Cartesian coordinate system, the _____ is represented on the x axis (or abscissa.)

a. BIBO stability
b. BDDC
c. 15 theorem
d. Domain

6. In mathematics, the _____ of a complex number z, is the second element of the ordered pair of real numbers representing z, i.e. if z = (x,y), or equivalently, z = x + iy, then the _____ of z is y. It is denoted by Im(z) or $\Im\{z\}$, where $\Im$ is a capital I in the Fraktur typeface. The complex function which maps z to the _____ of z is not holomorphic.

a. ALGOR
b. ACTRAN
c. Imaginary unit
d. Imaginary part

7. In calculus, an _____ is the limit of a definite integral as an endpoint of the interval of integration approaches either a specified real number or ∞ or −∞ or, in some cases, as both endpoints approach limits.

Specifically, an _____ is a limit of the form

$$\lim_{b\to\infty} \int_a^b f(x)\,dx, \qquad \lim_{a\to-\infty} \int_a^b f(x)\,dx,$$

or of the form

$$\lim_{c\to b^-} \int_a^c f(x)\,dx, \qquad \lim_{c\to a^+} \int_c^b f(x)\,dx,$$

in which one takes a limit in one or the other (or sometimes both) endpoints . Improper integrals may also occur at an interior point of the domain of integration, or at multiple such points.

a. AUSM
b. Improper integral
c. ACTRAN
d. ALGOR

8. Integration is an important concept in mathematics, specifically in the field of calculus and, more broadly, mathematical analysis. Given a function f of a real variable x and an interval [a, b] of the real line, the _____

$$\int_a^b f(x)\,dx,$$

is defined informally to be the net signed area of the region in the xy-plane bounded by the graph of $f$, the x-axis, and the vertical lines x = a and x = b.

The term '_____' may also refer to the notion of antiderivative, a function F whose derivative is the given function $f$.

    a. Integral
    b. Integrand
    c. Indefinite integral
    d. Integral test for convergence

9. In mathematics, the _____ of a function y = f(x) is a function that, in some fashion, 'undoes' the effect of f The _____ of f is denoted $f^{-1}$. The statements y=f(x) and x=$f^{-1}$(y) are equivalent.
    a. ALGOR
    b. ACTRAN
    c. AUSM
    d. Inverse

10. Let S be a set with a binary operation * . If e is an identity element of (S, * ) and a * b = e, then a is called a _____ of b and b is called a right inverse of a. If an element x is both a _____ and a right inverse of y, then x is called a two-sided inverse, or simply an inverse, of y.
    a. Hurwitz quaternion order
    b. Completing the square
    c. Closed-form expression
    d. Left inverse

11. An injective function is called an injection, and is also said to be a _____ function (not to be confused with _____ correspondence, i.e. a bijective function.)

A function f that is not injective is sometimes called many-to-one. (However, this terminology is also sometimes used to mean 'single-valued', i.e. each argument is mapped to at most one value.)

a. Onto
b. One-to-one function
c. Injective function
d. One-to-one

12. In mathematics, the _____ of a function is the set of all 'output' values produced by that function. Sometimes it is called the image, or more precisely, the image of the domain of the function. If a function is a surjection then its _____ is equal to its codomain.
   a. Surjective
   b. Range
   c. Constant function
   d. Piecewise-defined function

13. In mathematics, the _____ of a complex number z, is the first element of the ordered pair of real numbers representing z, i.e. if z = (x,y), or equivalently, z = x + iy, then the _____ of z is x. It is denoted by Re{z} or $\mathfrak{R}${z}, where $\mathfrak{R}$ is a capital R in the Fraktur typeface. The complex function which maps z to the _____ of z is not holomorphic.
   a. Conjugated line
   b. Complex number
   c. Real part
   d. Filled Julia set

14. In elementary mathematics, physics, and engineering, a _____ is a geometric object that has both a magnitude (or length), direction and sense, (i.e., orientation along the given direction.) A _____ is frequently represented by a line segment with a definite direction, or graphically as an arrow, connecting an initial point A with a terminal point B, and denoted by

$\overrightarrow{x}$.

The magnitude of the _____ is the length of the segment and the direction characterizes the displacement of B relative to A: how much one should move the point A to 'carry' it to the point B.

Many algebraic operations on real numbers have close analogues for vectors.

   a. BDDC
   b. 15 theorem
   c. Linear partial differential operator
   d. Vector

15. In mathematics, _____ and minima, known collectively as extrema, are the largest value (maximum) or smallest value (minimum), that a function takes in a point either within a given neighbourhood (local extremum) or on the function domain in its entirety (global extremum.)

Throughout, a point refers to an input (x), while a value refers to an output (y): one distinguishing between the maximum value and the point (or points) at which it occurs.

A real-valued function f defined on the real line is said to have a local maximum point at the point $x^*$, if there exists some $\varepsilon > 0$, such that $f(x^*) \geq f(x)$ when $|x - x^*| < \varepsilon$.

    a. Leibniz formula
    b. Racetrack principle
    c. Related rates
    d. Maxima

16. In mathematics, the _____ is a binary operation on two vectors in a three-dimensional Euclidean space that results in another vector which is perpendicular to the plane containing the two input vectors. The algebra defined by the _____ is neither commutative nor associative. It contrasts with the dot product which produces a scalar result.

    a. Permutation
    b. 15 theorem
    c. Fundamental theorem of algebra
    d. Cross product

17. In real analysis, the _____ is a fundamental result about convergence in a finite-dimensional Euclidean space $R^n$. The theorem states that each bounded sequence in $R^n$ has a convergent subsequence. An equivalent formulation is that a subset of $R^n$ is sequentially compact if and only if it is closed and bounded.

    a. Bolzano-Weierstrass theorem
    b. 15 theorem
    c. Multiplicative calculus
    d. Piecewise linear function

18. In mathematics, a function f defined on some set X with real or complex values is a _____ function, if the set of its values is _____. In other words, there exists a number M>0 such that

$$|f(x)| \leq M$$

for all x in X.

Sometimes, if $f(x) \leq A$ for all x in X, then the function is said to be _____ above by A.

a. Differential coefficient
b. Concave upwards
c. Stationary phase approximation
d. Bounded


19. A _____ is perfectly round geometrical object in three-dimensional space, such as the shape of a round ball. Like a circle in two dimensions, a perfect _____ is completely symmetrical around its center, with all points on the surface lying the same distance r from the center point. This distance r is known as the radius of the _____.
  a. Tangent line
  b. North pole
  c. Minimal surface
  d. Sphere


20. In topology, the boundary of a subset S of a topological space X is the set of points which can be approached both from S and from the outside of S. More formally, it is the set of points in the closure of S, not belonging to the interior of S. An element of the boundary of S is called a _____ of S. S is boundaryless when it contains no boundary, which is to say no _____ Notations used for boundary of a set S include bd(S), fr(S), and ∂S. Some authors (for example Willard, in General Topology) use the term 'frontier', instead of boundary in an attempt to avoid confusion with the concept of boundary used in algebraic topology.
  a. Boundary point
  b. 15 theorem
  c. BIBO stability
  d. BDDC


21. In mathematics, the interior of a set S consists of all points of S that are intuitively 'not on the edge of S'. A point that is in the interior of S is an _____ of S.

The exterior of a set is the interior of its complement; it consists of the points that are not in the set or its boundary.

  a. ACTRAN
  b. Interior point
  c. AUSM
  d. ALGOR

22. In mathematics, the concept of a '_____' is used to describe the behavior of a function as its argument or input either 'gets close' to some point, or as the argument becomes arbitrarily large; or the behavior of a sequence's elements as their index increases indefinitely. Limits are used in calculus and other branches of mathematical analysis to define derivatives and continuity.

In formulas, _____ is usually abbreviated as lim

   a. 15 theorem
   b. BIBO stability
   c. Limit
   d. BDDC

23. In mathematics, the _____ is a fundamental concept in calculus and analysis concerning the behavior of that function near a particular input. Informally, a function assigns an output f(x) to every input x. The function has a limit L at an input p if f(x) is 'close' to L whenever x is 'close' to p.

   a. Limit of a function
   b. 15 theorem
   c. Squeeze Theorem
   d. Table of limits

24. In mathematics, a _____ is an ordered list of objects (or events). Like a set, it contains members (also called elements or terms), and the number of terms (possibly infinite) is called the length of the _____. Unlike a set, order matters, and the exact same elements can appear multiple times at different positions in the _____.

   a. Y-intercept
   b. 15 theorem
   c. Sequence
   d. Slope

25. Cantor defined two kinds of _____ numbers, the ordinal numbers and the cardinal numbers. Ordinal numbers may be identified with well-ordered sets, or counting carried on to any stopping point, including points after an _____ number have already been counted. Generalizing finite and the ordinary _____ sequences which are maps from the positive integers leads to mappings from ordinal numbers, and transfinite sequences.

   a. ACTRAN
   b. AUSM
   c. ALGOR
   d. Infinite

## Chapter 1. Setting the Stage

26. In vector calculus, the _____ is an operator that measures the magnitude of a vector field's source or sink at a given point; the _____ of a vector field is a (signed) scalar. For example, consider air as it is heated or cooled. The relevant vector field for this example is the velocity of the moving air at a point.
   a. Green's theorem
   b. Divergence
   c. Gradient theorem
   d. Triple product

27. In mathematics, especially in order theory, an upper bound of a subset S of some partially ordered set (P, ≤) is an element of P which is greater than or equal to every element of S. The term _____ is defined dually as an element of P which is lesser than or equal to every element of S. A set with an upper bound is said to be bounded from above by that bound, a set with a _____ is said to be bounded from below by that bound.

A subset S of a partially ordered set P may fail to have any bounds or may have many different upper and lower bounds. By transitivity, any element greater than or equal to an upper bound of S is again an upper bound of S, and any element lesser than or equal to any _____ of S is again a _____ of S. This leads to the consideration of least upper bounds: (or suprema) and greatest lower bounds (or infima.)
   a. BIBO stability
   b. 15 theorem
   c. Lower bound
   d. BDDC

28. In mathematics, given a subset S of a partially ordered set T, the _____ (sup) of S, if it exists, is the least element of T that is greater than or equal to each element of S. Consequently, the _____ is also referred to as the least upper bound, lub or LUB. If the _____ exists, it may or may not belong to S.
   a. 15 theorem
   b. BDDC
   c. Supremum
   d. BIBO stability

29. In mathematics, especially in order theory, an _____ of a subset S of some partially ordered set (P, >≤) is an element of P which is greater than or equal to every element of S. The term lower bound is defined dually as an element of P which is lesser than or equal to every element of S. A set with an _____ is said to be bounded from above by that bound, a set with a lower bound is said to be bounded from below by that bound.

A subset S of a partially ordered set P may fail to have any bounds or may have many different upper and lower bounds. By transitivity, any element greater than or equal to an _____ of S is again an _____ of S, and any element lesser than or equal to any lower bound of S is again a lower bound of S. This leads to the consideration of least upper bounds: (or suprema) and greatest lower bounds (or infima.)

a. AUSM
b. ACTRAN
c. Upper bound
d. ALGOR

30. The largest and the smallest element of a set are called extreme values, absolute extrema, or extreme records.

For a differentiable function f, if f($x_0$) is an _____ for the set of all values f(x), and if $x_0$ is in the interior of the domain of f, then $x_0$ is a critical point, by Fermat's theorem.

In the case of a general partial order one should not confuse a least element (smaller than all other) and a minimal element (nothing is smaller.)

a. Integration by substitution
b. Extreme value
c. Infinitesimal
d. Extreme Value Theorem

31. In calculus, the _____ states that if a real-valued function f is continuous in the closed and bounded interval [a,b], then f must attain its maximum and minimum value, each at least once. That is, there exist numbers c and d in [a,b] such that:

$$f(c) \geq f(x) \geq f(d) \quad \text{for all } x \in [a, b].$$

A related theorem is the boundedness theorem which states that a continuous function f in the closed interval [a,b] is bounded on that interval. That is, there exist real numbers m and M such that:

$$m \leq f(x) \leq M \quad \text{for all } x \in [a, b].$$

The _____ enriches the boundedness theorem by saying that not only is the function bounded, but it also attains its least upper bound as its maximum and its greatest lower bound as its minimum.

a. Uniform convergence
b. Infinitesimal
c. Extreme value theorem
d. Integral of secant cubed

32. In mathematical analysis, the _____ states that for each value between the least upper bound and greatest lower bound of the image of a continuous function there is a corresponding value in its domain mapping to the original. _____

- Version I. The _____ states the following: If the function y = f(x) is continuous on the interval [a, b], and u is a number between f(a) and f(b), then there is a c ∈ [a, b] such that f(c) = u.

- Version II. Suppose that I is an interval [a, b] in the real numbers R and that f : I → R is a continuous function. Then the image set f(I) is also an interval, and either it contains [f(a), f(b)], or it contains [f(b), f(a)]; that is,

    f(I) ⊇ [f(a), f(b)], or f(I) ⊇ [f(b), f(a)].

It is frequently stated in the following equivalent form: Suppose that f : [a, b] → R is continuous and that u is a real number satisfying f(a) < u < f(b) or f(a) > u > f(b).) Then for some c ∈ [a, b], f(c) = u.

This captures an intuitive property of continuous functions: given f continuous on [1, 2], if f(1) = 3 and f(2) = 5 then f must take the value 4 somewhere between 1 and 2.

a. AUSM
b. ALGOR
c. ACTRAN
d. Intermediate value theorem


33. A _____ is a set of standard clothing worn by members of an organization while participating in that organization's activity. Modern uniforms are worn by armed forces and paramilitary organisations such as police, emergency services, security guards, in some workplaces and schools and by inmates in prisons. In some countries, some other officials also wear uniforms in their duties; such is the case of the Commissioned Corps of the United States Public Health Service or the French prefects.

a. AUSM
b. ACTRAN
c. Uniform
d. ALGOR


34. In mathematics, a function $f$ is uniformly continuous if, roughly speaking, it is possible to guarantee that $f(x)$ and $f(y)$ be as close to each other as we please by requiring only that x and y are sufficiently close to each other; unlike ordinary continuity, the maximum distance between $f(x)$ and $f(y)$ cannot depend on x and y themselves. For instance, any isometry (distance-preserving map) between metric spaces is uniformly continuous.

_____, unlike continuity, is meaningless in an arbitrary topological space, since it relies on the ability to compare the sizes of neighbourhoods of distinct points of a space.

a. Uniform continuity
b. AUSM
c. ACTRAN
d. ALGOR

## Chapter 2. Differential Calculus

1. In calculus, a branch of mathematics, the _____ is a measurement of how a function changes when its input changes. Loosely speaking, a _____ can be thought of as how much a quantity is changing at some given point. For example, the _____ of the position (or distance) of a vehicle with respect to time is the instantaneous velocity (respectively, instantaneous speed) at which the vehicle is traveling.

   The process of finding a _____ is called differentiation. The fundamental theorem of calculus states that differentiation is the reverse process to integration.

   a. Stationary phase approximation
   b. Semi-differentiability
   c. Bounded function
   d. Derivative

2. f'(x) is twice the absolute value function, and it does not have a derivative at zero. Similar examples show that a function can have k derivatives for any non-negative integer k but no (k + 1)-order derivative. A function that has k successive derivatives is called _____.
   a. Differential coefficient
   b. K times differentiable
   c. Power series
   d. Differential calculus

3. In mathematics, a _____ is a method for approximating the total area underneath a curve on a graph, otherwise known as an integral. It may also be used to define the integration operation.

   Consider a function $f: D \to \mathbf{R}$, where $D$ is a subset of the real numbers $\mathbf{R}$, and let $I = [a, b]$ be a closed interval contained in $D$. A finite set of points $\{x_0, x_1, x_2, \ldots x_n\}$ such that $a = x_0 < x_1 < x_2 \ldots < x_n = b$ creates a partition

   $$P = \{[x_0, x_1), [x_1, x_2), \ldots [x_{n-1}, x_n]\}$$

   of $I$.

   a. Signed measure
   b. Risch algorithm
   c. Solid of revolution
   d. Riemann sum

4. In mathematics, a _____ is a function which preserves the given order. This concept first arose in calculus, and was later generalized to the more abstract setting of order theory.

## Chapter 2. Differential Calculus

In calculus, a function f defined on a subset of the real numbers with real values is called monotonic (also monotonically increasing or non-decreasing), if for all x and y such that x >≤ y one has f(x) >≤ f(y), so f preserves the order.

   a. Monotonic function
   b. Pseudo-differential operator
   c. Pettis integral
   d. 15 theorem


5. In probability theory and statistics, the _____ (or expectation value or mean and for continuous random variables with a density function it is the probability density -weighted integral of the possible values.

The term '_____' can be misleading.

   a. ALGOR
   b. AUSM
   c. ACTRAN
   d. Expected value


6. In calculus, the _____ states, roughly, that given a section of a smooth curve, there is at least one point on that section at which the derivative (slope) of the curve is equal (parallel) to the 'average' derivative of the section. It is used to prove theorems that make global conclusions about a function on an interval starting from local hypotheses about derivatives at points of the interval.

This theorem can be understood concretely by applying it to motion: If a car travels one hundred miles in one hour, so its average speed during that time was 100 miles per hour.

   a. Periodic function
   b. Hyperbolic angle
   c. Limits of integration
   d. Mean value theorem


7. In geometry, the _____ (or simply the tangent) to a curve at a given point is the straight line that 'just touches' the curve at that point (in the sense explained more precisely below.) As it passes through the point of tangency, the _____ is 'going in the same direction' as the curve, and in this sense it is the best straight-line approximation to the curve at that point. The same definition applies to space curves and curves in n-dimensional Euclidean space.

a. Minimal surface
b. North pole
c. Lie derivative
d. Tangent line


8. In physics, _____ is defined as the rate of change of position. it is vector physical quantity; both speed and direction are required to define it. In the SI (metric) system, it is measured in meters per second: (m/s) or ms$^{-1}$.

a. BDDC
b. 15 theorem
c. BIBO stability
d. Velocity


9. In mathematics, a _____ of a function of several variables is its derivative with respect to one of those variables with the others held constant (as opposed to the total derivative, in which all variables are allowed to vary.) Partial derivatives are useful in vector calculus and differential geometry.

The _____ of a function f with respect to the variable x is written as $f'_x$, $\partial_x f$, or $\partial f/\partial x$.

a. Level curve
b. Differentiation operator
c. Jacobian
d. Partial derivative


10. In vector calculus, the _____ of a scalar field is a vector field which points in the direction of the greatest rate of increase of the scalar field, and whose magnitude is the greatest rate of change.

A generalization of the _____ for functions on a Euclidean space which have values in another Euclidean space is the Jacobian. A further generalization for a function from one Banach space to another is the Fréchet derivative.

a. Lin-Tsien equation
b. Symmetric derivative
c. Smooth function
d. Gradient

## Chapter 2. Differential Calculus

11. In infinitesimal calculus, a _____ is traditionally an infinitesimally small change in a variable. For example, if x is a variable, then a change in the value of x is often denoted Δx (or δx when this change is considered to be small.) The _____ dx represents such a change, but is infinitely small.

   a. Differential
   b. The Method of Mechanical Theorems
   c. Dirichlet integral
   d. Local maximum

12. In mathematics, the _____ of a multivariate differentiable function along a given vector V at a given point P intuitively represents the instantaneous rate of change of the function, moving through P, in the direction of V. It therefore generalizes the notion of a partial derivative, in which the direction is always taken parallel to one of the coordinate axes.

The _____ is a special case of the Gâteaux derivative.

The _____ of a scalar function $f(\vec{x}) = f(x_1, x_2, \ldots, x_n)$ along a vector $\vec{v} = (v_1, \ldots, v_n)$ is the function defined by the limit

$$<_____> \nabla_{\vec{v}} f(\vec{x}) = \lim_{h \to 0} \frac{f(\vec{x} + h\vec{v}) - f(\vec{x})}{h}.$$

Sometimes authors write $D_v$ instead of $\nabla_v$.

   a. Linearity of differentiation
   b. Symmetrically continuous
   c. Differentiation of trigonometric functions
   d. Directional derivative

13. In a totally ordered set all elements are mutually comparable, so such a set can have at most one minimal element and at most one maximal element. Then, due to mutual comparability, the minimal element will also be the least element and the maximal element will also be the greatest element. Thus in a totally ordered set we can simply use the terms minimum and _____.

   a. Racetrack principle
   b. Leibniz rule
   c. Nth term
   d. Maximum

14. In calculus, the _____ is a formula for the derivative of the composite of two functions.

In intuitive terms, if a variable, y, depends on a second variable, u, which in turn depends on a third variable, x, then the rate of change of y with respect to x can be computed as the rate of change of y with respect to u multiplied by the rate of change of u with respect to x. Schematically,

$$\frac{dy}{dx} = \frac{dy}{du} \cdot \frac{du}{dx}.$$

a. Chain rule
b. Differentiation rules
c. Reciprocal Rule
d. Product rule

15. In differential geometry there are a number of second-order, linear, elliptic differential operators bearing the name _____

The connection _____ is a differential operator acting on the various tensor bundles of a manifold, defined in terms of a Riemmanian- or pseudo-Riemannian metric.

a. Peetre theorem
b. Semi-elliptic operator
c. Dirac operator
d. Laplacian

16. In calculus, _____ gives a sequence of approximations of a differentiable function around a given point by polynomials (the Taylor polynomials of that function) whose coefficients depend only on the derivatives of the function at that point. The theorem also gives precise estimates on the size of the error in the approximation. The theorem is named after the mathematician Brook Taylor, who stated it in 1712, though the result was first discovered 41 years earlier in 1671 by James Gregory.
a. Local minimum
b. Related rates
c. Fresnel integrals
d. Taylor's theorem

17. Integration is an important concept in mathematics, specifically in the field of calculus and, more broadly, mathematical analysis. Given a function $f$ of a real variable x and an interval [a, b] of the real line, the _____

$$\int_a^b f(x)\,dx,$$

is defined informally to be the net signed area of the region in the xy-plane bounded by the graph of $f$, the x-axis, and the vertical lines x = a and x = b.

The term '_____' may also refer to the notion of antiderivative, a function F whose derivative is the given function $f$.

 a. Integral test for convergence
 b. Indefinite integral
 c. Integrand
 d. Integral


18. In mathematics, a _____ (or critical number) is a point on the domain of a function where:

- one dimension: the derivative (or slope of the line when visualized) is equal to zero or a point where the function ceases to be differentiable.
- in general: there are two distinct concepts: either the derivative (Jacobian) vanishes, or it is not of full rank (or, in either case, the function is not differentiable); these agree in one dimension.

Note that in one dimension, a critical value or critical number x of function f is the domain element at which the derivative is zero or undefined, whereas the associated ordered pair (x, y) is the _____. In higher dimensions a critical value is in the range whereas a _____ is in the domain.

There are two situations in which a point becomes a _____ of a function of one variable. The first of which is that the value of the first derivative is equal to zero.

 a. Differentiation operator
 b. Multivariable calculus
 c. Total derivative
 d. Critical point


19. A real-valued function f defined on the real line is said to have a _____ point at the point $x^*$, if there exists some $\varepsilon > 0$, such that $f(x^*) \geq f(x)$ when $|x - x^*| < \varepsilon$. The value of the function at this point is called maximum of the function.

On a graph of a function, its local maxima will look like the tops of hills.

a. Standard part function
b. Racetrack principle
c. Test for Divergence
d. Local maximum

20. In a totally ordered set all elements are mutually comparable, so such a set can have at most one minimal element and at most one maximal element. Then, due to mutual comparability, the minimal element will also be the least element and the maximal element will also be the greatest element. Thus in a totally ordered set we can simply use the terms _____ and maximum.
   a. Nth term
   b. Maximum
   c. Ghosts of departed quantities
   d. Minimum

21. In mathematics, a _____ is a point in the domain of a function of two variables which is a stationary point but not a local extremum. At such a point, in general, the surface resembles a saddle that curves up in one direction, and curves down in a different direction (like a mountain pass.) In terms of contour lines, a _____ can be recognized, in general, by a contour that appears to intersect itself.
   a. 15 theorem
   b. BDDC
   c. BIBO stability
   d. Saddle point

22. In mathematical optimization, the method of Lagrange multipliers provides a strategy for finding the maximum/minimum of a function subject to constraints.

For example , consider the optimization problem

$$\text{maximize } f(x, y)$$
$$\text{subject to } g(x, y) = c.$$

We introduce a new variable (λ) called a _____, and study the Lagrange function defined by

$$\Lambda(x, y, \lambda) = f(x, y) - \lambda\big(g(x, y) - c\big).$$

If (x,y)â‰ is a maximum for the original constrained problem, then there exists a λ such that (x,y,λ)â‰ is a stationary point for the Lagrange function (stationary points are those points where the partial derivatives of Λ are zero.) However, not all stationary points yield a solution of the original problem.

a. BIBO stability
b. BDDC
c. 15 theorem
d. Lagrange multiplier

23. The method of _____ or ordinary _____ is used to solve overdetermined systems. _____ is often applied in statistical contexts, particularly regression analysis.

_____ can be interpreted as a method of fitting data. The best fit in the _____ sense is that instance of the model for which the sum of squared residuals has its least value, a residual being the difference between an observed value and the value given by the model.

a. BDDC
b. 15 theorem
c. BIBO stability
d. Least squares

24. In vector calculus, the _____ is shorthand for either the _____ matrix or its determinant, the _____ determinant.

In algebraic geometry the _____ of a curve means the _____ variety: a group variety associated to the curve, in which the curve can be embedded.

These concepts are all named after the mathematician Carl Gustav Jacob Jacobi.

a. Jacobian
b. Vector Laplacian
c. Critical point
d. Saddle surface

## Chapter 3. The Implicit Function Theorem and Its Applications

1. In mathematics, an _____ is a generalization for the concept of a function in which the dependent variable has not been given 'explicitly' in terms of the independent variable. To give a function f explicitly is to provide a prescription for determining the output value of the function y in terms of the input value x:

   y = f(x.)

   By contrast, the function is implicit if the value of y is obtained from x by solving an equation of the form:

   R(x,y) = 0.

   a. Ordinary differential equation
   b. Implicit differentiation
   c. Automatic differentiation
   d. Implicit function

2. In the branch of mathematics called multivariable calculus, the _____ is a tool which allows relations to be converted to functions. It does this by representing the relation as the graph of a function. There may not be a single function whose graph is the entire relation, but there may be such a function on a restriction of the domain of the relation.
   a. Implicit function theorem
   b. Upper convected time derivative
   c. Isoperimetric inequality
   d. Inverse function theorem

3. In mathematics, a (topological) _____ is defined as follows: let I be an interval of real numbers (i.e. a non-empty connected subset of $\mathbb{R}$); then a _____ $\gamma$ is a continuous mapping $\gamma : I \to X$, where X is a topological space. The _____ $\gamma$ is said to be simple if it is injective, i.e. if for all x, y in I, we have $\gamma(x) = \gamma(y) \implies x = y$. If I is a closed bounded interval $[a, b]$, we also allow the possibility $\gamma(a) = \gamma(b)$ (this convention makes it possible to talk about closed simple _____.)
   a. Prolate cycloid
   b. Closed curve
   c. Tractrix
   d. Curve

4. A _____ is a type of manifold that is locally similar enough to Euclidean space to allow one to do calculus Any manifold can be described by a collection of charts, also known as an atlas.

## Chapter 3. The Implicit Function Theorem and Its Applications

a. Sphere
b. Tangent line
c. Minimal surface
d. Differentiable manifold

5. A _____ is a cubic curve generated by increasing or diminishing the radius vector of a variable point P on a straight line by the distance PA of the point from the foot of the perpendicular drawn from the origin to the fixed line.

The polar equation is

$$r = a\ \cos 2\theta \sec \theta.$$

The Cartesian equation is

$$y^2 = x^2 /,$$

where a is the distance of the line from the origin.

a. Strophoid
b. Dolbeault operator
c. Macbeath surface
d. Kampyle of Eudoxus

## Chapter 4. Integral Calculus

1. In mathematics, a _____ is a method for approximating the total area underneath a curve on a graph, otherwise known as an integral. It may also be used to define the integration operation.

Consider a function $f: D \rightarrow \mathbf{R}$, where $D$ is a subset of the real numbers $\mathbf{R}$, and let $I = [a, b]$ be a closed interval contained in $D$. A finite set of points $\{x_0, x_1, x_2, ... x_n\}$ such that $a = x_0 < x_1 < x_2 ... < x_n = b$ creates a partition

$$P = \{[x_0, x_1), [x_1, x_2), ... [x_{n-1}, x_n]\}$$

of $I$.

  a. Riemann sum
  b. Risch algorithm
  c. Signed measure
  d. Solid of revolution


2. In the branch of mathematics known as real analysis, the _____, created by Bernhard Riemann, was the first rigorous definition of the integral of a function on an interval. While the _____ is unsuitable for many theoretical purposes, it is one of the easiest integrals to define. Some of these technical deficiencies can be remedied by the Riemann-Stieltjes integral, and most of them disappear in the Lebesgue integral.
  a. Regulated integral
  b. Lebesgue integration
  c. Skorokhod integral
  d. Riemann integral


3. Integration is an important concept in mathematics, specifically in the field of calculus and, more broadly, mathematical analysis. Given a function $f$ of a real variable x and an interval [a, b] of the real line, the _____

$$\int_a^b f(x)\, dx,$$

is defined informally to be the net signed area of the region in the xy-plane bounded by the graph of $f$, the x-axis, and the vertical lines x = a and x = b.

The term '_____' may also refer to the notion of antiderivative, a function F whose derivative is the given function $f$.

a. Integral test for convergence
b. Indefinite integral
c. Integrand
d. Integral

4. The _____ specifies the relationship between the two central operations of calculus, differentiation and integration.

The first part of the theorem, sometimes called the first _____, shows that an indefinite integration can be reversed by a differentiation.

The second part, sometimes called the second _____, allows one to compute the definite integral of a function by using any one of its infinitely many antiderivatives.

a. Fundamental theorem of calculus
b. Leibniz formula
c. Periodic function
d. Limits of integration

5. In potential theory, the _____ is an integral kernel, used for solving the two-dimensional Dirichlet problem. Specifically, it gives solutions to the two-dimensional Laplace equation, given Dirichlet boundary conditions and circular symmetry. The kernel can be understood as the derivative of the Green's function for the Laplace equation.
a. BDDC
b. BIBO stability
c. 15 theorem
d. Poisson kernel

6. In probability theory and statistics, the _____ (or expectation value or mean and for continuous random variables with a density function it is the probability density -weighted integral of the possible values.

The term '_____' can be misleading.

a. ACTRAN
b. AUSM
c. Expected value
d. ALGOR

7. The _____ of a material is defined as its mass per unit volume. The symbol of _____ is ρ '>rho.)

Mathematically:

$$d = \frac{m}{V}$$

where:

    d is the _____,
    m is the mass,
    V is the volume.

  a. BIBO stability
  b. Density
  c. 15 theorem
  d. BDDC


8. In geometry, the _____, geometric center, or barycenter of a plane figure X is the intersection of all straight lines that divide X into two parts of equal moment about the line. Informally, it is the 'average' of all points of X. The definition extends to any object X in n-dimensional space: its _____ is the intersection of all hyperplanes that divide X into two parts of equal moment.
  a. 15 theorem
  b. BIBO stability
  c. BDDC
  d. Centroid


9. The concept of _____ in mathematics evolved from the concept of _____ in physics. The nth _____ of a real-valued function f(x) of a real variable about a value c is

$$\mu'_n = \int_{-\infty}^{\infty} (x-c)^n f(x)\, dx.$$

It is possible to define moments for random variables in a more general fashion than moments for real values. See Moments in metric spaces.

  a. Poisson distribution
  b. Median
  c. Geometric mean
  d. Moment

10. In mathematics and its applications, a _____ system is a system for assigning an n-tuple of numbers or scalars to each point in an n-dimensional space. This concept is part of the theory of manifolds. 'Scalars' in many cases means real numbers, but, depending on context, can mean complex numbers or elements of some other commutative ring.
   a. Cylindrical coordinate system
   b. Spherical coordinate system
   c. 15 theorem
   d. Coordinate

11. A _____ is one of the most curvilinear basic geometric shapes:It has two faces, zero vertices, and zero edges. The surface formed by the points at a fixed distance from a given straight line, the axis of the _____. The solid enclosed by this surface and by two planes perpendicular to the axis is also called a _____.
   a. Cylinder
   b. Right circular cylinder
   c. BDDC
   d. 15 theorem

12. If a particular point on a sphere is (arbitrarily) designated as its _____, then the corresponding antipodal point is called the south pole and the equator is the great circle that is equidistant to them. Great circles through the two poles are called lines (or meridians) of longitude, and the line connecting the two poles is called the axis of rotation. Circles on the sphere that are parallel to the equator are lines of latitude.
   a. Sphere
   b. Tangent line
   c. North pole
   d. Minimal surface

13. In real analysis, the _____ is a fundamental result about convergence in a finite-dimensional Euclidean space $R^n$. The theorem states that each bounded sequence in $R^n$ has a convergent subsequence. An equivalent formulation is that a subset of $R^n$ is sequentially compact if and only if it is closed and bounded.
   a. Multiplicative calculus
   b. Bolzano-Weierstrass theorem
   c. Piecewise linear function
   d. 15 theorem

14. In mathematics, a function f defined on some set X with real or complex values is a _____ function, if the set of its values is _____. In other words, there exists a number M>0 such that

$$|f(x)| \leq M$$

for all x in X.

Sometimes, if $f(x) \leq A$ for all x in X, then the function is said to be _____ above by A.

a. Concave upwards
b. Stationary phase approximation
c. Differential coefficient
d. Bounded


15. In calculus, an _____ is the limit of a definite integral as an endpoint of the interval of integration approaches either a specified real number or ∞ or −∞ or, in some cases, as both endpoints approach limits.

Specifically, an _____ is a limit of the form

$$\lim_{b \to \infty} \int_a^b f(x)\,dx, \qquad \lim_{a \to -\infty} \int_a^b f(x)\,dx,$$

or of the form

$$\lim_{c \to b^-} \int_a^c f(x)\,dx, \qquad \lim_{c \to a^+} \int_c^b f(x)\,dx,$$

in which one takes a limit in one or the other (or sometimes both) endpoints . Improper integrals may also occur at an interior point of the domain of integration, or at multiple such points.

a. Improper integral
b. ACTRAN
c. AUSM
d. ALGOR


16. In considering complex multiple-valued functions in complex analysis, the _____ of a function are the values along one chosen branch of that function, so it is single-valued.

Consider the complex logarithm function log z. It is defined as the complex number w such that

$$e^w = z$$

Now, for example, say we wish to find log i.

a. Cayley transform
b. Branch point
c. Mellin transform
d. Principal values

## Chapter 5. Line and Surface Integrals; Vector Analysis

1. In elementary mathematics, physics, and engineering, a _____ is a geometric object that has both a magnitude (or length), direction and sense, (i.e., orientation along the given direction.) A _____ is frequently represented by a line segment with a definite direction, or graphically as an arrow, connecting an initial point A with a terminal point B, and denoted by

> 

The magnitude of the _____ is the length of the segment and the direction characterizes the displacement of B relative to A: how much one should move the point A to 'carry' it to the point B.

Many algebraic operations on real numbers have close analogues for vectors.

  a. BDDC
  b. Linear partial differential operator
  c. 15 theorem
  d. Vector


2. In mathematics a _____ is a construction in vector calculus which associates a vector to every point in a (locally) Euclidean space.

Vector fields are often used in physics to model, for example, the speed and direction of a moving fluid throughout space, or the strength and direction of some force, such as the magnetic or gravitational force, as it changes from point to point.

In the rigorous mathematical treatment, (tangent) vector fields are defined on manifolds as sections of a manifold's tangent bundle.

  a. BDDC
  b. 15 theorem
  c. BIBO stability
  d. Vector field


3. For some curves there is a smallest number L that is an upper bound on the length of any polygonal approximation. If such a number exists, then the curve is said to be rectifiable and the curve is defined to have _____ L.

Let C be a curve in Euclidean (or, generally, a metric) space $X = R^n$, so C is the image of a continuous function $f : [a, b] \to X$ of the interval [a, b] into X.

a. Integration by parametric derivatives
b. Integrand
c. Arc length
d. Order of integration

4. _____ is the long dimension of any object. The _____ of a thing is the distance between its ends, its linear extent as measured from end to end. This may be distinguished from height, which is vertical extent, and width or breadth, which are the distance from side to side, measuring across the object at right angles to the _____.
   a. 15 theorem
   b. Length
   c. BIBO stability
   d. BDDC

5. In mathematics, a (topological) _____ is defined as follows: let I be an interval of real numbers (i.e. a non-empty connected subset of $\mathbb{R}$); then a _____ $\gamma$ is a continuous mapping $\gamma : I \to X$, where X is a topological space. The _____ $\gamma$ is said to be simple if it is injective, i.e. if for all x, y in I, we have $\gamma(x) = \gamma(y) \implies x = y$. If I is a closed bounded interval $[a, b]$, we also allow the possibility $\gamma(a) = \gamma(b)$ (this convention makes it possible to talk about closed simple _____.)
   a. Closed curve
   b. Tractrix
   c. Prolate cycloid
   d. Curve

6. In mathematics, an _____ on a real vector space is a choice of which ordered bases are 'positively' oriented and which are 'negatively' oriented. In the three-dimensional Euclidean space, the two possible basis orientations are called right-handed and left-handed (or right-chiral and left-chiral), respectively. However, the choice of _____ is independent of the handedness or chirality of the bases (although right-handed bases are typically declared to be positively oriented, they may also be assigned a negative _____.)
   a. Unit vector
   b. Orientation
   c. ALGOR
   d. ACTRAN

7. In mathematics, a _____ is a function whose definition is dependent on the value of the independent variable. Mathematically, a real-valued function f of a real variable x is a relationship whose definition is given differently on disjoint subsets of its domain

The word piecewise is also used to describe any property of a _____ that holds for each piece but may not hold for the whole domain of the function.

a. Piecewise-defined function
b. Constant function
c. Surjective
d. Range

8. Integration is an important concept in mathematics, specifically in the field of calculus and, more broadly, mathematical analysis. Given a function $f$ of a real variable x and an interval [a, b] of the real line, the _____

$$\int_a^b f(x)\,dx,$$

is defined informally to be the net signed area of the region in the xy-plane bounded by the graph of $f$, the x-axis, and the vertical lines x = a and x = b.

The term '_____' may also refer to the notion of antiderivative, a function F whose derivative is the given function $f$.

a. Indefinite integral
b. Integrand
c. Integral test for convergence
d. Integral

9. In mathematics, a _____ is an integral where the function to be integrated is evaluated along a curve. Various different line integrals are in use. A specific case of an integration along a closed curve in two dimensions or the complex plane is the contour integral.
a. Line integral
b. Picard theorem
c. Mittag-Leffler star
d. Radius of convergence

10. In infinitesimal calculus, a _____ is traditionally an infinitesimally small change in a variable. For example, if x is a variable, then a change in the value of x is often denoted Δx (or δx when this change is considered to be small.) The _____ dx represents such a change, but is infinitely small.

# Chapter 5. Line and Surface Integrals; Vector Analysis

   a. Local maximum
   b. Differential
   c. Dirichlet integral
   d. The Method of Mechanical Theorems

11. In the mathematical fields of differential geometry and tensor calculus, differential forms are an approach to multivariable calculus that is independent of coordinates. A _____ of degree k, or (differential) k-form, on a smooth manifold M is a smooth section of the kth exterior power of the cotangent bundle of M. The set of all k-forms on M is a vector space commonly denoted $\Omega^k(M)$.

A differential 0-form is by definition a smooth function on M. A differential 1-form is an object dual to a vector field on M.

   a. Two-form
   b. Hodge dual
   c. Soldering
   d. Differential form

12. In calculus, an _____ is the limit of a definite integral as an endpoint of the interval of integration approaches either a specified real number or ∞ or −∞ or, in some cases, as both endpoints approach limits.

Specifically, an _____ is a limit of the form

$$\lim_{b \to \infty} \int_a^b f(x)\,dx, \qquad \lim_{a \to -\infty} \int_a^b f(x)\,dx,$$

or of the form

$$\lim_{c \to b^-} \int_a^c f(x)\,dx, \qquad \lim_{c \to a^+} \int_c^b f(x)\,dx,$$

in which one takes a limit in one or the other (or sometimes both) endpoints. Improper integrals may also occur at an interior point of the domain of integration, or at multiple such points.

   a. Improper integral
   b. ACTRAN
   c. ALGOR
   d. AUSM

## Chapter 5. Line and Surface Integrals; Vector Analysis

13. In real analysis, the _____ is a fundamental result about convergence in a finite-dimensional Euclidean space $R^n$. The theorem states that each bounded sequence in $R^n$ has a convergent subsequence. An equivalent formulation is that a subset of $R^n$ is sequentially compact if and only if it is closed and bounded.

    a. 15 theorem
    b. Bolzano-Weierstrass theorem
    c. Multiplicative calculus
    d. Piecewise linear function

14. In potential theory, the _____ is an integral kernel, used for solving the two-dimensional Dirichlet problem. Specifically, it gives solutions to the two-dimensional Laplace equation, given Dirichlet boundary conditions and circular symmetry. The kernel can be understood as the derivative of the Green's function for the Laplace equation.

    a. BDDC
    b. 15 theorem
    c. BIBO stability
    d. Poisson kernel

15. A curve $\gamma$ is said to be closed or a loop if $I = [a, b]$ and if $\gamma(a) = \gamma(b)$. A _____ is thus a continuous mapping of the circle $S^1$; a simple _____ is also called a Jordan curve or a Jordan arc. The Jordan curve theorem states that such curves divide the plane into an 'interior' and an 'exterior'.

    a. Bullet-nose curve
    b. Curve
    c. Kappa curve
    d. Closed curve

16. In calculus, a branch of mathematics, the _____ is a measurement of how a function changes when its input changes. Loosely speaking, a _____ can be thought of as how much a quantity is changing at some given point. For example, the _____ of the position (or distance) of a vehicle with respect to time is the instantaneous velocity (respectively, instantaneous speed) at which the vehicle is traveling.

    The process of finding a _____ is called differentiation. The fundamental theorem of calculus states that differentiation is the reverse process to integration.

    a. Bounded function
    b. Derivative
    c. Stationary phase approximation
    d. Semi-differentiability

## Chapter 5. Line and Surface Integrals; Vector Analysis

17. In the various subfields of physics, there exist two common usages of the term _____, both with rigorous mathematical frameworks.

- In the study of transport phenomena (heat transfer, mass transfer and fluid dynamics), _____ is defined as the amount that flows through a unit area per unit time. _____ in this definition is a vector.
- In the field of electromagnetism and mathematics, _____ is usually the integral of a vector quantity over a finite surface. The result of this integration is a scalar quantity. The magnetic _____ is thus the integral of the magnetic vector field B over a surface, and the electric _____ is defined similarly. Using this definition, the _____ of the Poynting vector over a specified surface is the rate at which electromagnetic energy flows through that surface. Confusingly, the Poynting vector is sometimes called the power _____, which is an example of the first usage of _____, above. It has units of watts per square metre (WÂ·m$^{-2}$)

One could argue, based on the work of James Clerk Maxwell, that the transport definition precedes the more recent way the term is used in electromagnetism. The specific quote from Maxwell is 'In the case of fluxes, we have to take the integral, over a surface, of the _____ through every element of the surface. The result of this operation is called the surface integral of the _____.

a. Flux
b. BDDC
c. 15 theorem
d. BIBO stability


18. In mathematics, a _____ is an ordered list of objects (or events). Like a set, it contains members (also called elements or terms), and the number of terms (possibly infinite) is called the length of the _____. Unlike a set, order matters, and the exact same elements can appear multiple times at different positions in the _____.

a. Sequence
b. 15 theorem
c. Slope
d. Y-intercept


19. In mathematics, a _____ is a definite integral taken over a surface (which may be a curved set in space); it can be thought of as the double integral analog of the line integral. Given a surface, one may integrate over it scalar fields (that is, functions which return numbers as values), and vector fields (that is, functions which return vectors as values.)

Surface integrals have applications in physics, particularly with the classical theory of electromagnetism.

a. Symmetry of second derivatives
b. Differential operator
c. Surface integral
d. Contact

## Chapter 5. Line and Surface Integrals; Vector Analysis

20. In differential geometry there are a number of second-order, linear, elliptic differential operators bearing the name _____

The connection _____ is a differential operator acting on the various tensor bundles of a manifold, defined in terms of a Riemmanian- or pseudo-Riemannian metric.

a. Laplacian
b. Peetre theorem
c. Dirac operator
d. Semi-elliptic operator


21. In vector calculus, the _____ is an operator that measures the magnitude of a vector field's source or sink at a given point; the _____ of a vector field is a (signed) scalar. For example, consider air as it is heated or cooled. The relevant vector field for this example is the velocity of the moving air at a point.

a. Triple product
b. Gradient theorem
c. Green's theorem
d. Divergence


22. In vector calculus, the _____ Ostrogradskye;s theorem the _____ states that the outward flux of a vector field through a surface is equal to the triple integral of the divergence on the region inside the surface. Intuitively, it states that the sum of all sources minus the sum of all sinks gives the net flow out of a region.

a. Del
b. Divergence theorem
c. Divergence
d. Green's theorem


23. The _____ is an important partial differential equation which describes the distribution of heat (or variation in temperature) in a given region over time. For a function u(x,y,z,t) of three spatial variables (x,y,z) and the time variable t, the _____ is

$$\frac{\partial u}{\partial t} - k\left(\frac{\partial^2 u}{\partial x^2} + \frac{\partial^2 u}{\partial y^2} + \frac{\partial^2 u}{\partial z^2}\right) = 0$$

or equivalently

$$\frac{\partial u}{\partial t} = k\nabla^2 u$$

where k is a constant.

The _____ is of fundamental importance in diverse scientific fields.

  a. Heat equation
  b. 15 theorem
  c. BIBO stability
  d. BDDC


24. The _____ is an important second-order linear partial differential equation that describes the propagation of a variety of waves, such as sound waves, light waves and water waves. It arises in fields such as acoustics, electromagnetics, and fluid dynamics. Historically, the problem of a vibrating string such as that of a musical instrument was studied by Jean le Rond d'Alembert, Leonhard Euler, Daniel Bernoulli, and Joseph-Louis Lagrange.
  a. Volume
  b. Wave equation
  c. Lagrangian
  d. Dirac equation


25. In vector calculus a _____ is a vector field which is the gradient of a scalar potential. There are two closely related concepts: path independence and irrotational vector fields. Every _____ has zero curl (and is thus irrotational), and every _____ has the path independence property.
  a. Divergence Theorem
  b. Green's theorem
  c. Conservative vector field
  d. Del


26. In vector calculus, a _____ is a vector field whose curl is a given vector field. This is analogous to a scalar potential, which is a scalar field whose negative gradient is a given vector field.

Formally, given a vector field v, a _____ is a vector field A such that

$$\mathbf{v} = \nabla \times \mathbf{A}.$$

If a vector field v admits a _____ A, then from the equality

$$\nabla \cdot (\nabla \times \mathbf{A}) = 0$$

(divergence of the curl is zero) one obtains

$$\nabla \cdot \mathbf{v} = \nabla \cdot (\nabla \times \mathbf{A}) = 0,$$

which implies that v must be a solenoidal vector field.

a. Moment of Inertia
b. Wave equation
c. Vector potential
d. Lagrangian


27. _____ is a type of motion in which the velocity of an object changes equal amounts in equal time periods. An example of an object having _____ would be a ball rolling down a ramp. The object picks up velocity as it goes down the ramp with equal changes in time.

a. ALGOR
b. AUSM
c. ACTRAN
d. Uniform Acceleration


28. In differential geometry, the _____ extends the concept of the differential of a function, which is a form of degree zero, to differential forms of higher degree. Its current form was invented by Élie Cartan.

The _____ d has the property that $d^2 = 0$ and is the differential (coboundary) used to define de Rham (and Alexander-Spanier) cohomology on forms.

a. AUSM
b. ACTRAN
c. ALGOR
d. Exterior derivative

# Chapter 6. Infinite Series

1. Cantor defined two kinds of _____ numbers, the ordinal numbers and the cardinal numbers. Ordinal numbers may be identified with well-ordered sets, or counting carried on to any stopping point, including points after an _____ number have already been counted. Generalizing finite and the ordinary _____ sequences which are maps from the positive integers leads to mappings from ordinal numbers, and transfinite sequences.
   a. AUSM
   b. ALGOR
   c. ACTRAN
   d. Infinite

2. The terms of the series are often produced according to a certain rule, such as by a formula, by an algorithm, by a sequence of measurements, or even by a random number generator. As there are an infinite number of terms, this notion is often called an _____. Unlike finite summations, series need tools from mathematical analysis to be fully understood and manipulated.
   a. Integration by substitution
   b. Extreme Value Theorem
   c. Extreme value
   d. Infinite series

3. Integration is an important concept in mathematics, specifically in the field of calculus and, more broadly, mathematical analysis. Given a function $f$ of a real variable x and an interval [a, b] of the real line, the _____

$$\int_a^b f(x)\,dx,$$

is defined informally to be the net signed area of the region in the xy-plane bounded by the graph of $f$, the x-axis, and the vertical lines x = a and x = b.

The term '_____' may also refer to the notion of antiderivative, a function F whose derivative is the given function $f$.

   a. Indefinite integral
   b. Integral test for convergence
   c. Integrand
   d. Integral

4. Call $S_N$ the _____ to N of the sequence $\{a_n\}$, or _____ of the series. A series is the sequence of partial sums, $\{S_N\}$.

## Chapter 6. Infinite Series

When talking about series, one can refer either to the sequence $\{S_N\}$ of the partial sums, or to the sum of the series,

$$\sum_{n=0}^{\infty} a_n$$

i.e., the limit of the sequence of partial sums - it is clear which one is meant from context.

a. Partial sum
b. Maxima
c. The Method of Mechanical Theorems
d. Dirichlet integral

5. The _____ of an angle is the ratio of the length of the opposite side to the length of the hypotenuse. In our case

$$\sin A = \frac{\text{opposite}}{\text{hypotenuse}} = \frac{a}{h}.$$

Note that this ratio does not depend on size of the particular right triangle chosen, as long as it contains the angle A, since all such triangles are similar.

The cosine of an angle is the ratio of the length of the adjacent side to the length of the hypotenuse.

a. Sine integral
b. Trigonometric functions
c. Trigonometric
d. Sine

6. In mathematics, a _____ is a series with a constant ratio between successive terms. For example, the series

$$\frac{1}{2} + \frac{1}{4} + \frac{1}{8} + \frac{1}{16} + \cdots$$

is geometric, because each term is equal to half of the previous term. The sum of this series is 1, as illustrated in the following picture:

_____ are one of the simplest examples of infinite series with finite sums.

a. Conditionally convergent
b. Sequence transformation
c. Converge absolutely
d. Geometric series

7. In mathematics, the _____ is a representation of a function as an infinite sum of terms calculated from the values of its derivatives at a single point. It may be regarded as the limit of the Taylor polynomials. If the series is centered at zero, the series is also called a Maclaurin series.
   a. BIBO stability
   b. BDDC
   c. Taylor series
   d. 15 theorem

8. In mathematics, a _____ is an informal expression referring to a series whose sum can be found by exploiting the circumstance that nearly every term cancels with either a succeeding or preceding term. Such a technique is also known as the method of differences.

For example, the series

$$\sum_{n=1}^{\infty} \frac{1}{n(n+1)}$$

simplifies as

$$\sum_{n=1}^{\infty} \frac{1}{n(n+1)} = \sum_{n=1}^{\infty} \left( \frac{1}{n} - \frac{1}{n+1} \right)$$
$$= \left(1 - \frac{1}{2}\right) + \left(\frac{1}{2} - \frac{1}{3}\right) + \cdots$$
$$= 1 + \left(-\frac{1}{2} + \frac{1}{2}\right) + \left(-\frac{1}{3} + \frac{1}{3}\right) + \cdots = 1.$$

Although telescoping can be a useful technique, there are pitfalls to watch out for:

$$0 = \sum_{n=1}^{\infty} 0 = \sum_{n=1}^{\infty} (1-1) = 1 + \sum_{n=1}^{\infty} (-1+1) = 1$$

is not correct because regrouping of terms is invalid unless the individual terms converge to 0; see Grandi's series.

## Chapter 6. Infinite Series

a. Sequence transformation
b. Geometric series
c. Converge absolutely
d. Telescoping series

9. In the branch of mathematics known as real analysis, the _____, created by Bernhard Riemann, was the first rigorous definition of the integral of a function on an interval. While the _____ is unsuitable for many theoretical purposes, it is one of the easiest integrals to define. Some of these technical deficiencies can be remedied by the Riemann-Stieltjes integral, and most of them disappear in the Lebesgue integral.

a. Regulated integral
b. Riemann integral
c. Skorokhod integral
d. Lebesgue integration

10. In calculus, an _____ is the limit of a definite integral as an endpoint of the interval of integration approaches either a specified real number or ∞ or −∞ or, in some cases, as both endpoints approach limits.

Specifically, an _____ is a limit of the form

$$\lim_{b\to\infty} \int_a^b f(x)\,dx, \qquad \lim_{a\to-\infty} \int_a^b f(x)\,dx,$$

or of the form

$$\lim_{c\to b^-} \int_a^c f(x)\,dx, \qquad \lim_{c\to a^+} \int_c^b f(x)\,dx,$$

in which one takes a limit in one or the other (or sometimes both) endpoints . Improper integrals may also occur at an interior point of the domain of integration, or at multiple such points.

a. ALGOR
b. AUSM
c. ACTRAN
d. Improper integral

11. In mathematics, the _____ for convergence is a method used to test infinite series of non-negative terms for convergence. An early form of the test of convergence was developed in India by Madhava in the 14th century, and by his followers at the Kerala School. In Europe, it was later developed by Maclaurin and Cauchy and is sometimes known as the Maclaurin-Cauchy test.

a. ALGOR
b. ACTRAN
c. AUSM
d. Integral test


12. In mathematics, the _____, sometimes called the direct _____ is a criterion for convergence or divergence of a series whose terms are real or complex numbers. The test determines convergence by comparing the terms of the series in question with those of a series whose convergence properties are known.

The _____ states that if the series

$$\sum_{n=1}^{\infty} b_n$$

is an absolutely convergent series and

$$|a_n| \leq |b_n|$$

for sufficiently large n , then the series

$$\sum_{n=1}^{\infty} a_n$$

converges absolutely.

a. Ratio test
b. Conditionally convergent
c. Telescoping series
d. Comparison test


13. In mathematics, the concept of a '_____' is used to describe the behavior of a function as its argument or input either 'gets close' to some point, or as the argument becomes arbitrarily large; or the behavior of a sequence's elements as their index increases indefinitely. Limits are used in calculus and other branches of mathematical analysis to define derivatives and continuity.

In formulas, _____ is usually abbreviated as lim

a. 15 theorem
b. BIBO stability
c. Limit
d. BDDC

14. A _____ is an expression which compares quantities relative to each other. The most common examples involve two quantities, but in theory any number of quantities can be compared. In mathematical terms, they are represented by separating each quantity with a colon, for example the _____ 2:3, which is read as the _____ 'two to three'.
    a. 15 theorem
    b. Y-intercept
    c. Sequence
    d. Ratio

15. In mathematics, the _____ is a test (or 'criterion') for the convergence of a series

$$\sum_{n=0}^{\infty} a_n$$

whose terms are real or complex numbers. The test was first published by Jean le Rond d'Alembert and is sometimes known as d'Alembert's _____. The test makes use of the number

()

in the cases where this limit exists.

    a. Ratio test
    b. Converge absolutely
    c. Geometric series
    d. Telescoping series

16. In mathematics, the _____ is a criterion for the convergence (a convergence test) of an infinite series

$$\sum_{n=1}^{\infty} a_n.$$

It is particularly useful in connection with power series.

## Chapter 6. Infinite Series

The _____ was developed first by Cauchy and so is sometimes known as the Cauchy _____ or Cauchy's radical test. The _____ uses the number

$$C = \limsup_{n\to\infty} \sqrt[n]{|a_n|},$$

where 'lim sup' denotes the limit superior, possibly ∞.

   a. Racetrack principle
   b. Mean Value Theorem
   c. Related rates
   d. Root test

17. In mathematics, a series (or sometimes also an integral) is said to converge absolutely if the sum (or integral) of the absolute value of the summand or integrand is finite.

More precisely, a real or complex-valued series $\sum_{n=0}^{\infty} a_n$ is said to converge absolutely if $\sum_{n=0}^{\infty} |a_n| < \infty.$

_____ is vitally important to the study of infinite series because on the one hand, it is strong enough that such series retain certain basic properties of finite sums -- the most important ones being rearrangement of the terms and convergence of products of two infinite series -- that are unfortunately not possessed by all convergent series. On the other hand _____ is weak enough to occur very often in practice.

   a. Eisenstein series
   b. ACTRAN
   c. Alternating series test
   d. Absolute convergence

18. _____ is a type of motion in which the velocity of an object changes equal amounts in equal time periods. An example of an object having _____ would be a ball rolling down a ramp. The object picks up velocity as it goes down the ramp with equal changes in time.
   a. ACTRAN
   b. AUSM
   c. ALGOR
   d. Uniform Acceleration

## Chapter 6. Infinite Series

19. In mathematics, an _____ is an infinite series of the form

$$\sum_{n=0}^{\infty}(-1)^n a_n,$$

with $a_n \geq 0$ (or $a_n \leq 0$) for all n. A finite sum of this kind is an alternating sum. An _____ converges if the terms $a_n$ converge to 0 monotonically.

    a. Uniform convergence
    b. Infinite series
    c. Extreme value
    d. Alternating series

20. The _____ is a method used to prove that infinite series of terms converge. It was discovered by Gottfried Leibniz and is sometimes known as Leibniz's test or the Leibniz criterion.

A series of the form

$$\sum_{n=1}^{\infty}(-1)^n a_n$$

where all the $a_n$ are positive or 0, is called an alternating series.

    a. Absolute convergence
    b. ACTRAN
    c. Alternating series test
    d. Eisenstein series

21. _____ is the addition of a set of numbers; the result is their sum or total. An interim or present total of a _____ process is termed the running total. The 'numbers' to be summed may be natural numbers, complex numbers, matrices, or still more complicated objects.
    a. BDDC
    b. 15 theorem
    c. BIBO stability
    d. Summation

# Chapter 7. Functions Defined by Series and Integrals

1. In mathematics, a _____ is an ordered list of objects (or events). Like a set, it contains members (also called elements or terms), and the number of terms (possibly infinite) is called the length of the _____. Unlike a set, order matters, and the exact same elements can appear multiple times at different positions in the _____.
   a. Y-intercept
   b. 15 theorem
   c. Sequence
   d. Slope

2. A _____ is a set of standard clothing worn by members of an organization while participating in that organization's activity. Modern uniforms are worn by armed forces and paramilitary organisations such as police, emergency services, security guards, in some workplaces and schools and by inmates in prisons. In some countries, some other officials also wear uniforms in their duties; such is the case of the Commissioned Corps of the United States Public Health Service or the French prefects.
   a. AUSM
   b. ACTRAN
   c. Uniform
   d. ALGOR

3. In the mathematical field of analysis, _____ is a type of convergence stronger than pointwise convergence. A sequence { $f_n$ } of functions converges uniformly to a limiting function f if the speed of convergence of $f_n(x)$ to f(x) does not depend on x.

   The concept is important because several properties of the functions $f_n$, such as continuity and Riemann integrability, are transferred to the limit f if the convergence is uniform.

   a. Even function
   b. Operational calculus
   c. Uniform convergence
   d. Extreme Value Theorem

4. In potential theory, the _____ is an integral kernel, used for solving the two-dimensional Dirichlet problem. Specifically, it gives solutions to the two-dimensional Laplace equation, given Dirichlet boundary conditions and circular symmetry. The kernel can be understood as the derivative of the Green's function for the Laplace equation.
   a. BDDC
   b. 15 theorem
   c. Poisson kernel
   d. BIBO stability

5. In mathematics, a _____ (in one variable) is an infinite series of the form

$$f(x) = \sum_{n=0}^{\infty} a_n (x-c)^n = a_0 + a_1(x-c)^1 + a_2(x-c)^2 + a_3(x-c)^3 + \cdots$$

where $a_n$ represents the coefficient of the nth term, c is a constant, and x varies around c (for this reason one sometimes speaks of the series as being centered at c

In many situations c is equal to zero, for instance when considering a Maclaurin series.

a. Stationary phase approximation
b. Differential calculus
c. Power series
d. Differential coefficient

6. In mathematics, the _____ of a power series is a non-negative quantity, either a real number or $\infty$, that represents a domain (within the radius) in which the series will converge. Within the _____, a power series converges absolutely and uniformly on compacta as well. If the series converges, it is the Taylor series of the analytic function to which it converges inside its _____.

a. Holomorphically separable
b. Blaschke product
c. Branch point
d. Radius of convergence

## Chapter 7. Functions Defined by Series and Integrals

7. In elementary algebra, a _____ is a polynomial with two terms--the sum of two monomials--often bound by parenthesis or brackets when operated upon. It is the simplest kind of polynomial other than monomials.

- The _____ $a^2 - b^2$ can be factored as the product of two other binomials:

    $a^2 - b^2 = (a + b)(a - b.)$

    This is a special case of the more general formula:

    $$a^{n+1} - b^{n+1} = (a - b) \sum_{k=0}^{n} a^k b^{n-k}$$

- The product of a pair of linear binomials (ax + b) and (cx + d) is:

    $(ax + b)(cx + d) = acx^2 + axd + bcx + bd.$

- A _____ raised to the n$^{th}$ power, represented as

    $(a + b)^n$

    can be expanded by means of the _____ theorem or, equivalently, using Pascal's triangle. Taking a simple example, the perfect square _____ $(p + q)^2$ can be found by squaring the :first digit, adding twice the product of the first and second digit and finally adding the square of the second digit, to give $p^2 + 2pq + q^2$.

a. Partial fractions
b. Completing the square
c. Binomial
d. Multinomial theorem


8. In mathematics, the _____ generalizes the purely algebraic formula of the binomial theorem to complex values of α. It is also a special case of a Newton series. The _____ is the series

$$(1 + x)^\alpha = \sum_{k=0}^{\infty} \binom{\alpha}{k} x^k = \sum_{k=0}^{\infty} \frac{\prod_{a=0}^{k-1}(\alpha - a) \, x^k}{k!}$$

where α is a complex number and

$$\binom{\alpha}{k} = \frac{\alpha(\alpha - 1)(\alpha - 2) \cdots (\alpha - k + 1)}{k!}$$

is the (generalized) binomial coefficient (if α is a non negative integer, then the (α + 1) th term and all later terms in the series are zero, since each one contains a factor equal to (α - α): thus, in that case, the summation reduces to the algebraic binomial formula.)

a. Maxima
b. Fresnel integrals
c. Binomial series
d. Differential


9. In mathematics, _____, first defined by the mathematician Daniel Bernoulli and generalized by Friedrich Bessel, are canonical solutions y(x) of Bessel's differential equation:

$$x^2 \frac{d^2 y}{dx^2} + x \frac{dy}{dx} + (x^2 - \alpha^2) y = 0$$

for an arbitrary real or complex number α (the order of the Bessel function.) The most common and important special case is where α is an integer n.

Although α and −α produce the same differential equation, it is conventional to define different _____ for these two orders (e.g., so that the _____ are mostly smooth functions of α.)

a. Multiplication theorem
b. 15 theorem
c. Logarithmic integral function
d. Bessel functions


10. In calculus, an _____ is the limit of a definite integral as an endpoint of the interval of integration approaches either a specified real number or ∞ or −∞ or, in some cases, as both endpoints approach limits.

Specifically, an _____ is a limit of the form

$$\lim_{b \to \infty} \int_a^b f(x)\,dx, \qquad \lim_{a \to -\infty} \int_a^b f(x)\,dx,$$

or of the form

$$\lim_{c \to b^-} \int_a^c f(x)\,dx, \qquad \lim_{c \to a^+} \int_c^b f(x)\,dx,$$

in which one takes a limit in one or the other (or sometimes both) endpoints . Improper integrals may also occur at an interior point of the domain of integration, or at multiple such points.

## Chapter 7. Functions Defined by Series and Integrals

a. AUSM
b. ALGOR
c. ACTRAN
d. Improper integral

11. Integration is an important concept in mathematics, specifically in the field of calculus and, more broadly, mathematical analysis. Given a function $f$ of a real variable x and an interval [a, b] of the real line, the _____

$$\int_a^b f(x)\,dx,$$

is defined informally to be the net signed area of the region in the xy-plane bounded by the graph of $f$, the x-axis, and the vertical lines x = a and x = b.

The term '_____' may also refer to the notion of antiderivative, a function F whose derivative is the given function $f$.

a. Indefinite integral
b. Integral test for convergence
c. Integrand
d. Integral

12. In mathematics, the _____ is an extension of the factorial function to real and complex numbers. For a complex number z with positive real part the _____ is defined by

$$\Gamma(z) = \int_0^\infty t^{z-1} e^{-t}\,dt\ .$$

This definition can be extended to the rest of the complex plane, excepting the non-positive integers.

If n is a positive integer, then

$\Gamma(n) = (n-1)!$,

showing the connection to the factorial function.

a. Digamma function
b. Pochhammer k-symbol
c. Gamma function
d. Multivariate gamma function

13. In mathematics, the _____, also called the Euler integral of the first kind, is a special function defined by

$$B(x, y) = \int_0^1 t^{x-1}(1-t)^{y-1}\, dt$$

for $\operatorname{Re}(x), \operatorname{Re}(y) > 0.$

The _____ was studied by Euler and Legendre and was given its name by Jacques Binet.

The _____ is symmetric, meaning that

$$B(x, y) = B(y, x).$$

It has many other forms, including:

$$B(x,y) = \frac{\Gamma(x)\Gamma(y)}{\Gamma(x+y)}$$

$$B(x,y) = 2\int_0^{\pi/2} (\sin\theta)^{2x-1}(\cos\theta)^{2y-1}\,d\theta, \qquad \mathrm{Re}(x) > 0,\ \mathrm{Re}(y) > 0$$

$$B(x,y) = \int_0^\infty \frac{t^{x-1}}{(1+t)^{x+y}}\,dt, \qquad \mathrm{Re}(x) > 0,\ \mathrm{Re}(y) > 0$$

$$B(x,y) = \sum_{n=0}^\infty \frac{\binom{n-y}{n}}{x+n},$$

$$B(x,y) = \prod_{n=0}^\infty \left(1 + \frac{xy}{n(x+y+n)}\right)^{-1},$$

$$B(x,y)\cdot B(x+y, 1-y) = \frac{\pi}{x\sin(\pi y)},$$

where $\Gamma$ is the gamma function. The second identity shows in particular $\Gamma(1/2) = \sqrt{\pi}$.

a. Pochhammer k-symbol
b. Pochhammer symbol
c. Multivariate gamma function
d. Beta function

14.  In calculus, a branch of mathematics, the _____ is a measurement of how a function changes when its input changes. Loosely speaking, a _____ can be thought of as how much a quantity is changing at some given point. For example, the _____ of the position (or distance) of a vehicle with respect to time is the instantaneous velocity (respectively, instantaneous speed) at which the vehicle is traveling.

The process of finding a _____ is called differentiation. The fundamental theorem of calculus states that differentiation is the reverse process to integration.

a. Bounded function
b. Stationary phase approximation
c. Semi-differentiability
d. Derivative

## Chapter 8. Fourier Series

1. In mathematics, a _____ is a function that repeats its values in regular intervals or periods. The most important examples are the trigonometric functions, which repeat over intervals of length 2π. Periodic functions are used throughout science to describe oscillations, waves, and other phenomena that exhibit periodicity.
    a. Partial sum
    b. Periodic function
    c. Limits of integration
    d. Term test


2. In mathematics, a _____ is a function whose definition is dependent on the value of the independent variable. Mathematically, a real-valued function f of a real variable x is a relationship whose definition is given differently on disjoint subsets of its domain

    The word piecewise is also used to describe any property of a _____ that holds for each piece but may not hold for the whole domain of the function.

    a. Range
    b. Constant function
    c. Surjective
    d. Piecewise-defined function


3. In mathematics, a _____ decomposes a periodic function into a sum of simple oscillating functions, namely sines and cosines (or complex exponentials.) The study of _____ is a branch of Fourier analysis. _____ were introduced by Joseph Fourier (1768-1830) for the purpose of solving the heat equation in a metal plate.
    a. 15 theorem
    b. BIBO stability
    c. BDDC
    d. Fourier series


4. In mathematics, a _____ is a constant multiplicative factor of a certain object. For example, in the expression $9x^2$, the _____ of $x^2$ is 9.

    The object can be such things as a variable, a vector, a function, etc.

    a. Degree of the polynomial
    b. Binomial type
    c. Resultant
    d. Coefficient

## Chapter 8. Fourier Series

5. In potential theory, the _____ is an integral kernel, used for solving the two-dimensional Dirichlet problem. Specifically, it gives solutions to the two-dimensional Laplace equation, given Dirichlet boundary conditions and circular symmetry. The kernel can be understood as the derivative of the Green's function for the Laplace equation.
   a. BDDC
   b. 15 theorem
   c. BIBO stability
   d. Poisson kernel

6. The _____ of an angle is the ratio of the length of the adjacent side to the length of the hypotenuse. In our case

$$\cos A = \frac{\text{adjacent}}{\text{hypotenuse}} = \frac{b}{h}.$$

The tangent of an angle is the ratio of the length of the opposite side to the length of the adjacent side. In our case

$$\tan A = \frac{\text{opposite}}{\text{adjacent}} = \frac{a}{b}.$$

The remaining three functions are best defined using the above three functions.

   a. Trigonometric functions
   b. Trigonometric
   c. Sine integral
   d. Cosine

7. The _____ of an angle is the ratio of the length of the opposite side to the length of the hypotenuse. In our case

$$\sin A = \frac{\text{opposite}}{\text{hypotenuse}} = \frac{a}{h}.$$

Note that this ratio does not depend on size of the particular right triangle chosen, as long as it contains the angle A, since all such triangles are similar.

The cosine of an angle is the ratio of the length of the adjacent side to the length of the hypotenuse.

a. Trigonometric
b. Trigonometric functions
c. Sine integral
d. Sine


8. The _____ is an important partial differential equation which describes the distribution of heat (or variation in temperature) in a given region over time. For a function u(x,y,z,t) of three spatial variables (x,y,z) and the time variable t, the _____ is

$$\frac{\partial u}{\partial t} - k\left(\frac{\partial^2 u}{\partial x^2} + \frac{\partial^2 u}{\partial y^2} + \frac{\partial^2 u}{\partial z^2}\right) = 0$$

or equivalently

$$\frac{\partial u}{\partial t} = k\nabla^2 u$$

where k is a constant.

The _____ is of fundamental importance in diverse scientific fields.

a. BIBO stability
b. Heat equation
c. 15 theorem
d. BDDC


9. In mathematics, _____ is any of several methods for solving ordinary and partial differential equations, in which algebra allows one to rewrite an equation so that each of two variables occurs on a different side of the equation.

Suppose a differential equation can be written in the form

$$\frac{d}{dx}f(x) = g(x)h(f(x)), \qquad (1)$$

which we can write more simply by letting y = f(x):

$$\frac{dy}{dx} = g(x)h(y).$$

## Chapter 8. Fourier Series

As long as h(y) ≠ 0, we can rearrange terms to obtain:

$$\frac{dy}{h(y)} = g(x)dx,$$

so that the two variables x and y have been separated.

Some who dislike Leibniz's notation may prefer to write this as

$$\frac{1}{h(y)}\frac{dy}{dx} = g(x),$$

but that fails to make it quite as obvious why this is called '_____'.

a. Damping ratio
b. Separation of variables
c. Power series method
d. Sturm separation theorem


10. The _____ is an important second-order linear partial differential equation that describes the propagation of a variety of waves, such as sound waves, light waves and water waves. It arises in fields such as acoustics, electromagnetics, and fluid dynamics. Historically, the problem of a vibrating string such as that of a musical instrument was studied by Jean le Rond d'Alembert, Leonhard Euler, Daniel Bernoulli, and Joseph-Louis Lagrange.

a. Dirac equation
b. Volume
c. Lagrangian
d. Wave equation


11. In mathematics, a _____ is the problem of finding a function which solves a specified partial differential equation (PDE) in the interior of a given region that takes prescribed values on the boundary of the region.

The _____ can be solved for many PDEs, although originally it was posed for Laplace's equation. In that case the problem can be stated as follows:

> Given a function f that has values everywhere on the boundary of a region in $R^n$, is there a unique continuous function u twice continuously differentiable in the interior and continuous on the boundary, such that u is harmonic in the interior and u = f on the boundary?

This requirement is called the Dirichlet boundary condition.

a. Quadrature domain
b. Pluripolar set
c. Dirichlet problem
d. Multipole expansion


12. In mathematics, the _____ gives an explicit solution to the Dirichlet problem for Laplace's equation in a ball in Euclidean space $R^n$.

If u is a harmonic function in the ball in $R^n$ centered at the origin with radius R, then the formula states

$$u(x) = \frac{R^2 - |x|^2}{\omega_n R} \int_{\partial B_R} \frac{u(y)}{|x-y|^n} dS(y)$$

where $\omega_n$ is the surface area of the unit sphere. The integration is performed over the surface of the ball, with unit surface area dS(y).

a. Homotopy principle
b. Spherical harmonics
c. Phase space method
d. Poisson integral formula


13. Integration is an important concept in mathematics, specifically in the field of calculus and, more broadly, mathematical analysis. Given a function $f$ of a real variable x and an interval [a, b] of the real line, the _____

$$\int_a^b f(x)\, dx,$$

is defined informally to be the net signed area of the region in the xy-plane bounded by the graph of $f$, the x-axis, and the vertical lines x = a and x = b.

The term '_____' may also refer to the notion of antiderivative, a function F whose derivative is the given function $f$.

a. Integral test for convergence
b. Integrand
c. Integral
d. Indefinite integral

14. In mathematics, an _____ space is a vector space with the additional structure of _____. This additional structure associates each pair of vectors in the space with a scalar quantity known as the _____ of the vectors. Inner products allow the rigorous introduction of intuitive geometrical notions such as the length of a vector or the angle between two vectors.
   a. Inner product
   b. AUSM
   c. ACTRAN
   d. ALGOR

15. In mathematics, two vectors are _____ if they are perpendicular, i.e., they form a right angle. For example, a subway and the street above, although they do not physically intersect, are _____ if they cross at a right angle.
   a. ACTRAN
   b. ALGOR
   c. AUSM
   d. Orthogonal

16. In mathematics, a _____ is an ordered list of objects (or events). Like a set, it contains members (also called elements or terms), and the number of terms (possibly infinite) is called the length of the _____. Unlike a set, order matters, and the exact same elements can appear multiple times at different positions in the _____.
   a. Slope
   b. 15 theorem
   c. Sequence
   d. Y-intercept

17. The _____ is a geometric inequality involving the square of the circumference of a closed curve in the plane and the area of a plane region it encloses, as well as its various generalizations. Isoperimetric literally means 'having the same perimeter'. The isoperimetric problem is to determine a plane figure of the largest possible area whose boundary has a specified length.
   a. Inverse function theorem
   b. Implicit function theorem
   c. Upper convected time derivative
   d. Isoperimetric inequality

18. In mathematics, _____ are a concept central to linear algebra and related fields of mathematics

Suppose that K is a field and V is a vector space over K. As usual, we call elements of V vectors and call elements of K scalars.

a. Linear combinations
b. Fundamental theorem of algebra
c. 15 theorem
d. Permutation

19. Let S be a set with a binary operation * . If e is an identity element of (S, * ) and a * b = e, then a is called a _____ of b and b is called a right inverse of a. If an element x is both a _____ and a right inverse of y, then x is called a two-sided inverse, or simply an inverse, of y.
   a. Completing the square
   b. Closed-form expression
   c. Hurwitz quaternion order
   d. Left inverse

20. In elementary mathematics, physics, and engineering, a _____ is a geometric object that has both a magnitude (or length), direction and sense, (i.e., orientation along the given direction.) A _____ is frequently represented by a line segment with a definite direction, or graphically as an arrow, connecting an initial point A with a terminal point B, and denoted by

The magnitude of the _____ is the length of the segment and the direction characterizes the displacement of B relative to A: how much one should move the point A to 'carry' it to the point B.

Many algebraic operations on real numbers have close analogues for vectors.

   a. BDDC
   b. Linear partial differential operator
   c. 15 theorem
   d. Vector

21. In calculus, an _____ is the limit of a definite integral as an endpoint of the interval of integration approaches either a specified real number or ∞ or −∞ or, in some cases, as both endpoints approach limits.

Specifically, an _____ is a limit of the form

$$\lim_{b \to \infty} \int_a^b f(x)\,dx, \qquad \lim_{a \to -\infty} \int_a^b f(x)\,dx,$$

or of the form

$$\lim_{c \to b^-} \int_a^c f(x)\,dx, \quad \lim_{c \to a^+} \int_c^b f(x)\,dx,$$

in which one takes a limit in one or the other (or sometimes both) endpoints . Improper integrals may also occur at an interior point of the domain of integration, or at multiple such points.

a. ACTRAN
b. ALGOR
c. Improper integral
d. AUSM


22.   In mathematics, _____ refers to the rewriting of an expression into a simpler form. For example, the process of rewriting a fraction into one with the smallest whole-number denominator possible (while keeping the numerator an integer) is called 'reducing a fraction'. Rewriting a radical (or 'root') expression with the smallest possible whole number under the radical symbol is called 'reducing a radical'.

a. Quartic
b. Reduction
c. 15 theorem
d. BDDC


23.   In algebra, a _____ is a function depending on n that associates a scalar, det(A), to an n×n square matrix A. The fundamental geometric meaning of a _____ is a scale factor for measure when A is regarded as a linear transformation. Determinants are important both in calculus, where they enter the substitution rule for several variables, and in multilinear algebra.

For a fixed nonnegative integer n, there is a unique _____ function for the n×n matrices over any commutative ring R. In particular, this function exists when R is the field of real or complex numbers.

a. 15 theorem
b. BIBO stability
c. BDDC
d. Determinant

# ANSWER KEY

**Chapter 1**
| | | | | | | | | | |
|---|---|---|---|---|---|---|---|---|---|
| 1. b | 2. a | 3. d | 4. d | 5. d | 6. d | 7. b | 8. a | 9. d | 10. d |
| 11. d | 12. b | 13. c | 14. d | 15. d | 16. d | 17. a | 18. d | 19. d | 20. a |
| 21. b | 22. c | 23. a | 24. c | 25. d | 26. b | 27. c | 28. c | 29. c | 30. b |
| 31. c | 32. d | 33. c | 34. a | | | | | | |

**Chapter 2**
| | | | | | | | | | |
|---|---|---|---|---|---|---|---|---|---|
| 1. d | 2. b | 3. d | 4. a | 5. d | 6. d | 7. d | 8. d | 9. d | 10. d |
| 11. a | 12. d | 13. d | 14. a | 15. d | 16. d | 17. d | 18. d | 19. d | 20. d |
| 21. d | 22. d | 23. d | 24. a | | | | | | |

**Chapter 3**
| | | | | |
|---|---|---|---|---|
| 1. d | 2. a | 3. d | 4. d | 5. a |

**Chapter 4**
| | | | | | | | | | |
|---|---|---|---|---|---|---|---|---|---|
| 1. a | 2. d | 3. d | 4. a | 5. d | 6. c | 7. b | 8. d | 9. d | 10. d |
| 11. a | 12. c | 13. b | 14. d | 15. a | 16. d | | | | |

**Chapter 5**
| | | | | | | | | | |
|---|---|---|---|---|---|---|---|---|---|
| 1. d | 2. d | 3. c | 4. b | 5. d | 6. b | 7. a | 8. d | 9. a | 10. b |
| 11. d | 12. a | 13. b | 14. d | 15. d | 16. b | 17. a | 18. a | 19. c | 20. a |
| 21. d | 22. b | 23. a | 24. b | 25. c | 26. c | 27. d | 28. d | | |

**Chapter 6**
| | | | | | | | | | |
|---|---|---|---|---|---|---|---|---|---|
| 1. d | 2. d | 3. d | 4. a | 5. d | 6. d | 7. c | 8. d | 9. b | 10. d |
| 11. d | 12. d | 13. c | 14. d | 15. a | 16. d | 17. d | 18. d | 19. d | 20. c |
| 21. d | | | | | | | | | |

**Chapter 7**
| | | | | | | | | | |
|---|---|---|---|---|---|---|---|---|---|
| 1. c | 2. c | 3. c | 4. c | 5. c | 6. d | 7. c | 8. c | 9. d | 10. d |
| 11. d | 12. c | 13. d | 14. d | | | | | | |

**Chapter 8**
| | | | | | | | | | |
|---|---|---|---|---|---|---|---|---|---|
| 1. b | 2. d | 3. d | 4. d | 5. d | 6. d | 7. d | 8. b | 9. b | 10. d |
| 11. c | 12. d | 13. c | 14. a | 15. d | 16. c | 17. d | 18. a | 19. d | 20. d |
| 21. c | 22. b | 23. d | | | | | | | |